How to Live and Why

Questions from the
Sermon on the Mount

Brian and Jordan Douglas

Copyright 2019, Brian Stanley Douglas and Jordan Nicole Douglas. All rights reserved.

ISBN: 978-0-578-47850-0

All biblical quotations are from the English Standard Version (ESV).

To Bryan and Nichol Starr

Thank you for following Jesus with us.
May we persevere to the end.

These questions began as a study at All Saints Presbyterian Church in the spring of 2018. They are formatted here for group or individual study.

We do not assume that the reader is a Christian. We hope this is useful to anyone who would take a closer look at what Jesus actually taught.

We were grateful to Bryan and Nichol Starr, who led the study with us and whose input shaped what you find here. Thanks also to John Erisman, who was in the study with us and always asks great questions.

One of the modern American church's greatest needs is to hear the Sermon on the Mount anew. These questions are a small contribution to that end. *Soli deo gloria.*

Brian and Jordan Douglas

Meridian, Idaho

January 2020

Week 1
Matthew 5:1-16

Who was the Sermon on the Mount originally meant for?

What is Jesus trying to accomplish through this sermon? Has its meaning changed in the time since?

Why should we study this Sermon?

What do you hope to receive from it?

Does the life described here seem attractive to you? Why or why not?

The Beatitudes: Matthew 5.2-12

What is the common theme in these verses? How would you summarize them all into one sentence?

Which of these seems most obvious or clear to you? Which seem unclear?

Which of these seems most difficult and why?

What does it mean to be "blessed"? How is that similar or different to happiness?

For many of these verses, there is a logical connection between the character trait and result. However, how do the meek inherit the earth?

How are each of these a blessing?
How does they add up to a blessed life?

In what ways do these verses contrast with what you have seen of how the world works? Does that change how you view them?

What is the Kingdom of Heaven, and who belongs to it? (see Matt 8.10-12 for further insight)

List some ways in which we are meant to actually <u>do</u> these?

Matthew 5.13-16

Where does the world need salt and light today? In what ways are we meant to provide it? Is there a risk of being too salty?

Who in your life has most embodied this teaching? In what specific places or relationships can you be salt and light this week?

Week 2
Matthew 5:17-26

The Law and the Prophets: Matthew 5.17-20

What does it mean to abolish the law? To fulfill? Contrast the two.

How did Jesus fulfill the law?
Where do we see that fulfillment in
the Sermon on the Mount?

How does this part of Jesus's sermon relate to the Beatitudes (Matthew 5.2-12)? What is the connection (if any)?

Does this passage require us to keep all of the Old Testament laws that were given to Israel? What is Jesus calling us to do here?

>(See Matthew 15.1-20; Acts 10.13; Galatians 5.2; Colossians 2.13.)

What do we learn about what God values from verse 19?

The Pharisees built their reputation on righteousness according to the law. How can our righteousness <u>exceed</u> that of the Pharisees?

Anger: Matthew 5.21-26

What do we learn about anger from verses 21-26? How does that fit with what we know about anger from society, psychology, or scripture?

Do you agree that anger is like murder? Why or why not? Is it ever okay to be angry?

How often are you angry, and how does your anger manifest itself? Is your anger more often constructive or destructive?

What makes you most angry?

What makes God angry?

How often do the two overlap?

What do we learn about the *value* of reconciliation from these verses?

What do we learn about our *method* for reconciliation from these verses?

Do you have any relationships that need reconciliation?

What is preventing that?

What steps can you take toward it?

Week 3
Matthew 5:27-37

Matthew 5.27-30: Lust

Why does Jesus connect lust and adultery? How are they similar or different?

Is Jesus teaching something new here? Was this the first time someone made that connection?

Does Jesus mean for us to take him literally in verses 29-30? Why does he choose to use this kind of graphic language? What did he want his hearers to do?

What causes you to sin?

What will you do about it?

Matthew 5.31-32: Divorce

Is Jesus teaching something new here? Was this the first time someone taught about divorce in this way?

How does this contrast with or challenge our cultural view of divorce? Which one most naturally resonates with us and why?

Matthew 5.33-37: Oaths

Jesus follows teaching about murder and adultery with teaching about oaths. Are these three equally important, or is he doing something different here?

Is Jesus prohibiting oaths? If so, then why do Christians still take them? If not, then what does he mean?

General Questions

How does Jesus challenge not only our actions, but also our motives and desires?

How does reading Matthew 5.20 affect our understanding of Jesus's "but I say to you" statements?

(see Matthew 5.22, 28, 32, 34, 39, 44)

What might have struck Jesus's original hearers as being different than their usual teachers? What conclusions can we draw about Jesus from this?

Does the "spirit" of these laws differ from the "letter"? What should guide our interpretation of them?

How can we view Jesus's teaching positively? That is, not just as "thou shalt not" prohibitions, but as a description of a better world and a more joyful life?

Think of your desires in relating to others: your spouse, coworkers, neighbors. In what ways is this challenging to you?

Week 4
Matthew 5:38-6:4

Matthew 5.38-42: Vengeance

Jesus is quoting from the Old Testament law in verse 38 (see Exodus 21.24; Leviticus 24.20; Deuteronomy 19.21). Is he contradicting the law? How do we understand this in light of in Matthew 5.18?

What is Jesus teaching about justice in verses 38-42? How does this challenge our idea of justice?

Can you think of an instance when revenge satisfied justice? What does this passage teach us about revenge?

When are you most tempted to resist this teaching, and why?

How does this inform our understanding of God's character? How should that shape our own character?

The radical giving described in verses 40 and especially 42 would change the resources we have for our family. How do we reconcile that tension?

"Think of the irritations and difficulties you regularly experience in your daily life. What would it mean to reflect God's generous love despite the pressure and provocation, despite your own anger and frustration?"

N.T. Wright, *Matthew for Everyone*

Matthew 5.43-48: Love your enemies

According to this passage, *why* are we to love our enemies?

What do we learn here about *how* to love our enemies? When do we find this easy to practice, and when is it difficult?

What does verse 48 mean, both in concept and in practice?

Matthew 6.1-4: Public vs. private

What does it mean to practice our righteousness before others?
What are its obvious forms, and which ones are more subtle?

What does Jesus say will happen if we practice righteousness before others? Why is that the penalty, and does it seem just?

When are you most tempted to practice righteousness before others?

What does Jesus say will happen if we practice righteousness in secret?
Does that motivate you?

What might practicing our righteousness in secret look like in practice? When does it come most naturally to you, and when is it most challenging?

How does Jesus embody his teaching in this passage? Are there any ways in which he doesn't?

Week 5
Matthew 6:5-15

Matthew 6.5-15: Prayer

What do verses 5-8 teach us about the God to whom we are praying? How should this be reflected in our prayers?

What false motives for prayer does Jesus identify, and what do they reveal about our beliefs about prayer?

Is there anything that you feel you must include in your prayers to make them more effective?

How does this passage apply?

Why does Jesus begin his prayer where he does?

What does it mean that God is our Father? Can you think of other places in the Bible (or elsewhere) that God is referred to as *Father?*

How does God's fatherhood change your prayers? Your worship?

What does hallowed mean? Can you think of other places in Scripture where someone hallows God's name?

How can we consciously hallow God's name in our prayers? At other times?

Why do we need Jesus's kingdom to come? Isn't it already here?

Why does Jesus teach his disciples to pray each of these specific petitions? How would you summarize each one?

Which petition is most needed in your own life?

When you read about Jesus's life, it's clear he loves prayer. Prayer is harder for us. How can we increase our love for prayer?

If we were writing verse 12, we might have asked for help in forgiving others, rather than stating it as done. In verses 14-15 it seems that the disciples still needed help in this area.

Why was verse 12 stated as if it were already true?

In what ways does God lead us/not lead us into temptation?

What does Jesus leave out of this prayer? Does that mean that those things are less important?

What words are repeated in the body of the prayer? Do any of these suggest a structure or theme?

How should you pray differently after reading this passage? What steps will you take to change your prayers?

Week 6
Matthew 6:16-34

Matthew 6.16-18: Fasting

What is the purpose of fasting or similar practices? What does it do for our humanity: body, mind, and soul?

Is fasting still relevant today?

If so, how?

Do you practice fasting?

Why and how?

Why is it important to not be "gloomy" while fasting?

Other than "rewards," why is secrecy important in fasting?

Matthew 6.19-24: Treasure in Heaven

Why does Jesus say we should not lay up earthly treasures? Do you agree with Jesus' valuation?

Can you think of any exceptions to this teaching?

What are heavenly treasures? In what ways are they superior to earthly ones? How can one store them up?

What are the "treasures" described? Do you think they are physical objects, or are they something intangible or spiritual?

Is verse 24 too extreme? Is "hate" too strong?

Is money bad? Is there a way to balance serving both God and money?

What is your treasure? What is it that you cannot get enough of? What are you leaning on for your joy? What makes you angry or afraid when you lose it?

Matthew 6.25-34: Anxiety

Telling someone not to worry is typically fruitless or even insulting. Is there a practical way we can help others worry less?

How can we worry less ourselves?

"Daily bread" is one of those expressions that perhaps sounds familiar, but we don't often really consider. What can we learn from that phrase, and what does it mean in 21st Century America?

What should we learn about work from the example of the birds? Are there any ways in which that lesson does <u>not</u> apply to human work?

What three things make you most anxious?

What does it mean to seek first the God's kingdom and righteousness? How are we to <u>do</u> that?

General Question

Which of the 10 Commandments do these sections (Matthew 6.16-34) have in common?

Week 7
Matthew 7:1-14

Matthew 7.1-6: Judging Others

The Greek word for "judge" [κρίνω, krino] was typically used in a legal sense. When Jesus said, "judge not, lest you be judged," what is he forbidding?

Can you think of other biblical passages about judgment? How do they help inform this one?

This passage is sometimes quoted to deflect critique. Is that a fair representation of what Jesus is teaching here? Why or why not?

Is Jesus implying that if we don't judge others, we will escape judgment?

In verse 5, Jesus seems to assume that we will remove specks from others' eyes. What does he mean by that? How are we to do so?

How will we know when we have adequately removed the plank from our own eye, so that we can remove the speck from others'?

How does verse 5 inform the rest of this passage?

Is verse 6 an interruption or continuation of verses 1-5? How does that affect how we read this section?

Who is Jesus referring to in verse 6?

What does he mean by this?

Matthew 7.7-11: Asking God

What is Jesus commanding in verse 7?

What does he promise?

When you don't get what you want,

should you ask harder?

How is God described in this passage?

Does that sound believable to you?

Why or why not?

How should you apply this teaching to your life today?

Matthew 7.12: The Golden Rule

Does the Golden Rule always apply?
Are there any exceptions?

How do "the Law and the Prophets" teach this principle?

If we followed this rule, what kind of life would that create?

Who do you most struggle to honor in this way? How will you work on that?

Week 8
Matthew 7:15-29

Matthew 7.13-14: The Narrow Way

How does the Golden Rule apply to verses 13-14?

Why is the way of destruction described as wide and easy? What makes the way of life narrow and harder to find?

Have you found the way of life?
How confident are you about your
answer and why?

Matthew 7.15-20: The Prophet's Fruit

How can we recognize false prophets?
What are their "fruits"?

Why should we beware them?

What is the danger?

How does this teaching fit with the beginning of chapter 7?

Matthew 7.21-23: Depart From Me

What is the danger here?

What are we meant to do about it?

Does this passage apply to you?

If so, in what way?

Should this passage cause us to question our salvation?
Why or why not?

Matthew 7.24-27: Two Houses

What are the two kinds of people in this passage? How will you recognize them?

What is the caution in this parable? How will you know whether you are "safe"?

Matthew 7.28-29: Jesus's Authority

Would you describe Jesus's teaching in the same way these crowds did? Why or why not?

What distinguishes the Sermon on the Mount from other teaching in the Bible? From the teaching of other faiths?

How will this sermon change your thoughts, actions, and desires?

About the Authors

Brian Douglas is a pastor at All Saints Presbyterian Church in Meridian, Idaho.

Jordan Douglas is a teacher at The Ambrose School in Meridian, Idaho.

They have been married since 2001 and have three children.

www.ingramcontent.com/pod-product-compliance
Lightning Source LLC
Chambersburg PA
CBHW021952290426
44108CB00012B/1040